STEFAN WAIDELICH

SOPHIE
AND THE
LOST COIN

ILLUSTRATED BY ALEXANDRA PULGA

Sophie and the lost coin

Imprint:
Authors: Stefan Waidelich, Sarah Schaufert
Illustrator: Alexandra Pulga

ISBN:
978-3-98661-097-5 Paperback
978-3-98661-098-2 Hardcover
978-3-98661-099-9 eBook

1st Edition - November 2023
© 2023 Stefan Waidelich, Zeisigweg 6, 72213 Altensteig

Cover illustration: Alexandra Pulga © Stefan Waidelich

For Sophie,
Emma
and Samuel

Sophie has been searching through the stinking garbage by the roadside for hours. "It's so hot," she sighs and sits down, exhausted.

What's that? There's a sparkle in the dirt. Curious, she reaches for the rusty piece of metal. What is it?

"A coin!" Sophie exclaims.
She grabs it and rushes
home as quickly as she can.
She must show her father!

Sophie's path leads through the narrow and dirty streets of Cebu City in the Philippines.
She lives with her father in one of the poorest neighborhoods.
6

«Daddy! Look! I found a treasure!» she cries out and proudly shows him the old coin.

Suddenly, a shadow falls on them. A raven flies
towards Sophie's hand and snatches the coin.

"No, don't!" Sophie screams desperately.
But the raven pays no attention.

He calmly flaps over a wall
and contentedly lands on the
balcony railing of a huge house.

"That's so mean!" Sophie is annoyed and stomps the floor.

She's been hunting for a treasure like this for ages. And now this stupid bird comes along and takes it right out of her hands.

"Getting angry won't help. We'll get your coin back," her father reassures her.

They walk quickly to the gate which leads into the huge house's yard.

There must be a way to get the coin back from the raven.

An elegantly dressed man appears on the
balcony. "Get out of here!" he yells, scaring the bird.
Croaking, the raven drops the coin and flies away.
    The rich man picks up the dirty coin and
looks at it closely.

Then he notices Sophie and her father outside his gate. He shouts at them rudely, "Get out of here, you beggars!"

Then he looks back and sees that the strangers are still there. Angrily, he calls for two guards, who immediately rush out.
Hurriedly, Sophie and her father flee.
14

Sophie watches as the rich man throws away her coin in disgust.

The coin lands on a rooftop, rolls off, and falls between the buildings.

15

"Dad, did you see that? He just threw the coin away!" gasps Sophie, stunned, as she and her father slow down.

"I'm sure he thought it was just a worthless piece of junk. Come on, we'll find the coin again!" replies her father firmly.

They reach the spot where they suspect the coin is and stop in astonishment.

The remains of a collapsed building lie in front of them.

"Wait for me here," says Sophie's father, carefully climbing over the rotten wooden planks and broken stones.

17

He makes his way forward, step by step. Finally, he sees a faint glimmer among the rubble. "I've found it!" he rejoices, grabbing the small coin. As he slowly walks back to Sophie, he stumbles.

Frightened, Sophie watches as
her father and her treasure end up
between the stones and planks.

"Did you hurt yourself?" cries Sophie in fear. As she tries to run towards him, a strong hand holds her. She turns slowly.

"Who do we have here? A dirty piggy
digging in the dirt?" a big boy sneers,
pushing Sophie onto the ground.

Silently, Sophie watches as three
more burly boys run up to her father.
"Look, the old man has brought us
a present," one of them calls out.
He picks up the coin that had
fallen from Sophie's father's hand.
Laughing, the boys throw the coin to
each other.

MABUHAY
TEAM

Sophie struggles to her feet.
She must do something!

Moving as quickly as
she can, she rams the boy
holding the coin. Out of
fright, he drops the coin.

Sophie tries to grab it. But it is too late. The coin falls into a small shaft.

"That's what comes of it!" the
boys yell and run off laughing.

Sobbing, Sophie sits in front of the grille.
How can people be so mean?

"Everything will be fine, darling."
Sophie's father struggles to his feet and
hobbles quickly to his daughter. He gives
her a comforting hug.

Once Sophie has calmed down, her father examines the shaft. It's impossible to get to the coin from where they are. "The opening ends in a sewer pipe," he remarks, looking around. In the distance, he sees a small river flowing. "Surely that's where it goes," says Sophie's father, limping towards it.

And indeed, the pipe ends in the river. Luckily, it is
dry inside and just big enough for Sophie to squeeze
in. Although scared, the little girl doesn't hesitate and
climbs into the narrow pipe with determination.

It's pitch-black inside, and it stinks terribly.
But from afar, Sophie sees a dim light. It is shining
through the opening where the coin fell in. Slowly, on
her hands and knees, Sophie crawls towards the light.
When she is finally under the hole, Sophie searches
the dark surroundings with her hands.

As she digs deep into the mud, Sophie grins and
exclaims, "I got you!" She wraps her fingers around
the dirty coin in relief. "Now, I just need to get out
of here!" Sophie thinks.

But can she turn around in this narrow tube?

Should she crawl backwards?
Suddenly, she hears a voice close to her.
"Sophie! Come to me!"

Relieved, Sophie recognizes her father's
voice and crawls forward.
That's when she sees
the end of the pipe.

Completely filthy but happy, Sophie squeezes out
and falls into her father's arms.

33

"We did it, Dad! I've found my treasure again," Sophie laughs and jumps in the air for joy.

But then she falls silent and looks sadly at the coin in her hand. After this adventure, her soiled treasure has become even dirtier. "Is my coin still valuable?" she asks her father anxiously.

"Of course it is!" he assures her. "A coin never loses its value, no matter how dirty it is."

35

Sophie's father takes his daughter on his lap. "Listen to me carefully, my little darling! Just as the coin never loses its value, you will always be precious. No matter what people say about you or do to you. It doesn't matter if you're dirty or feeling bad. You will always be valuable. Nothing in the world can ever change that."

Sophie's dad was right. The dirty piece of metal everyone treated with such scorn was indeed a treasure. The director of the city museum was amazed and wanted to exhibit the coin in his museum. "You can visit it anytime!" he promised, handing Sophie a bulging money case.

Since then, Sophie and her father have been able to afford everything they need.

They often visit the museum to see their big little treasure.

*"There is something precious in everyone that
is not in anyone else."*

—Martin Buber

Hey there, tiny treasure seeker,

Perhaps you relate to our friend Sophie, who sometimes feels alone or unappreciated. Maybe life's circumstances seem super tough, or perhaps some people poke fun at you or don't want to be your friend. No matter what happens, remember that you're precious and valuable, just as much as anyone else. You are unique and priceless, like Sophie's coin. No one, and I mean no one, can take this away from you. You are a real-life treasure!

Thank you for coming along on the journey. Did you enjoy it? If so, please share this message with the world. Everyone must know that they are unique and valuable. You can write about this story on social media or leave a review. This book could also be a perfect gift to inspire someone else.

Thanks for joining Sophie on this grand adventure. Who knows? Maybe we'll cross paths one day. That'd be really neat. I wish you all the very best and hope you realize just how special and priceless you truly are.

Best wishes,

Stefan Waidelich

P.S: The street kids in the Philippines face situations similar to, or tougher than, what Sophie went through. If you feel inspired to lend a helping hand, you can donate to the Christ for Asia organization. They work hard to care for these children who need help. Learn about their wonderful work by scanning the QR code on the next page.

About the Authors

Author:

Stefan Waidelich

is a math teacher. He lives in the Black Forest with his family, a cat, and six chickens. He loves stories, sports, God, and vanilla ice cream. He passionately believes everyone is valuable, no matter what they can do or have done, what they look like, or what they've been through.

Co-author:

Sarah Schaufert

lives in a small village in the Black Forest. She loves spending time with her family and being alone in the forest, where she enjoys nature and peace. She likes writing, painting, cuddling with her cats, eating chocolate, and listening to audiobooks.

Illustrator:

Alexandra Pulga

is a digital visionary from the Philippines, Alexandra paints with passion and imagination. She lives in her small city Tacloban where she fills her tiny world with people she loves, books, art, music, and more hobbies that she could ever count in both hands. As a wide-eyed dreamer, and with her observant eyes and intuitive nature, she creates vivid children's book worlds in which every child becomes a hero.